STAND UP!

You had to learn how to stand.
Standing up is a powerful thing.

You stand up so much now that I bet you don't even
think about it anymore. But let me ask you this.
Why did you stand up that very first time?

I bet you stood up to take that first
step toward your mom or dad.

We stand up for the things we love.

"STAND UP" means more than using your legs and feet. You can STAND UP to help your family, your friends, and your neighbors.

You can STAND UP for what you believe.

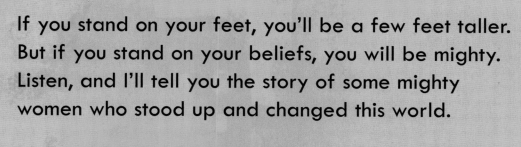

If you stand on your feet, you'll be a few feet taller. But if you stand on your beliefs, you will be mighty. Listen, and I'll tell you the story of some mighty women who stood up and changed this world.

MUM BETT

Mum Bett was born into slavery in Massachusetts around 1744.

She was enslaved her whole life, but after the American Revolution, she went to a public reading of the new Constitution. She heard the words, "All men are born free and equal."

So she thought to herself, "Why not me?"

Mum Bett took her owner to court. She asked the judge if the Constitution was just a bunch of pretty words or if it actually *meant* what it said.

And she won.

That's how she became the first enslaved person to be freed in the new country known as America, "the land of the free."

MUM BETT STOOD UP BY DEMANDING HER RIGHTS.

PHILLIS WHEATLEY

Phillis Wheatley was born in Africa.

But in 1761, at the age of eight, she was stolen from her family, chained on a ship, and sent to America.

She found herself in a strange new land, with a strange new language she had never heard before, and some of the leaders of America had a strange and terrible idea. They said a Black person was not a real person ("three-fifths of a man" is how they later put it). They said a Black person was property and could be enslaved. And that's what happened to her.

But Phillis Wheatley had an extraordinary mind.

Her owners recognized her talent and gave her an education. By age twelve, she learned to read and write in four different languages. She discovered poetry and how to express what she felt inside.

At fourteen, she wrote her first poem. At twenty, she published her first book. Phillis Wheatley became famous as America's first Black woman poet.

Her words showed that Black people are equal to everyone else.

PHILLIS WHEATLEY PICKED UP A PEN.
THAT'S HOW SHE TOOK A STAND.

IDA B. WELLS

Ida B. Wells was a writer.

She wanted America to know that slavery may have ended after the Civil War, but Black people were still not free.

They lived in terror of the night. That's when racist cowards hid their faces, and brought ropes and torches to let Black people know what would happen if they stood up or spoke out.

But Ida refused to be silent. In the 1890s, she started her own newspaper to tell the world about the terror in the night. Angry mobs destroyed her office and smashed her printing press, but Ida refused to back down.

She traveled the country, speaking and writing and organizing protests, letting racists know they could never hide from her pen.

IDA B. WELLS STOOD UP BY SPEAKING OUT.

ROSA PARKS

In 1955, in Montgomery, Alabama, the best swimming pools, the best water fountains, and the best seats on all the buses were reserved for "Whites Only."

No Black people allowed. This is called segregation.

Eventually, two women got fed up. They sat down in the Whites Only seats and got arrested because they refused to move. They went to jail, and inspired others to follow.

Lots of people know about Rosa Parks, who was tired after work and just wanted to go home. The story of her arrest sparked the Civil Rights Movement.

But not many know about Claudette Colvin.

CLAUDETTE COLVIN

Claudette did the same thing as Rosa Parks, but she did it nine months earlier. She was fifteen years old.

Claudette was a student on a bus coming home from a day at school, where she'd studied the history of Black women. She'd read about folks like Mum Bett and Ida B. Wells. That day, she decided to sit wherever she pleased, and she would not be moved.

ROSA PARKS AND CLAUDETTE COLVIN STOOD UP BY SITTING DOWN.

RUBY BRIDGES

In 1960, Ruby Bridges was a little girl, getting ready for her first day of school.

The school she was attending used to be segregated, but times had changed, and the law said it was okay for White and Black kids to be together.

Times may have changed, but old hatreds had not. When Ruby walked to school that first day, a crowd showed up and screamed at her to go home.

But Ruby Bridges ignored them all. She was only six years old, but Ruby Bridges was a giant that day and every day after. She dedicated her life to fighting for justice.

RUBY STOOD UP BY GOING TO SCHOOL.

PRATHIA HALL

In the 1960s, a Philadelphia preacher named Prathia Hall believed the best way to stand up in a democracy was to make every vote count.

She wanted to organize to help Black people vote. And one Sunday in church, she preached about what the world would look like if everyone was equal, and what a better place that would be.

She started with the words, "I have a dream..." The Reverend Martin Luther King Jr. was in that church and thought her words were so powerful that he carried them to the steps of the Lincoln Memorial, and on August 28, 1963, he preached them to the world.

PRATHIA HALL STOOD UP BY PREACHING OUT.

LELIA FOLEY

Lelia Foley isn't mentioned in any history books.

Then again, she never wanted to make history. All Lelia Foley wanted to do was improve her kids' school. So in 1973, she ran for election on her local school board.

She lost, but she didn't give up. She ran again, but this time she wanted to be mayor of the whole town . . . and she won! Lelia Foley became the first Black female mayor in American history.

THAT'S HOW LELIA FOLEY STOOD UP. SHE GOT OUT THE VOTE.

BREE NEWSOME

Bree Newsome is a documentary filmmaker from North Carolina.

Documentaries are movies about the real world. A filmmaker looks for powerful stories and images that affect our lives.

Bree saw one of those images flying over the capitol building of South Carolina. It was the Confederate flag—the symbol of the South during slavery. The Civil War ended 150 years ago. Slavery was outlawed. But that flag was still being displayed as if it were something to be proud of. To Bree, that image meant hatred and pain.

So Bree gave the world an image that was even more powerful. On June 27, 2015, she climbed that flagpole, and that was no small feat. It was thirty feet high!

She shouted, "This flag comes down today." And she slid down that pole with the Confederate flag crumpled in her hands. She was arrested and the flag went back up, but do you know what happened next?

The outpouring of support for Bree was so great that South Carolina was shamed into removing the flag for good.

BREE NEWSOME STOOD UP BY CLIMBING HIGH.

MARI COPENY

Mari Copeny is from the town of Flint, Michigan.

Every child in her neighborhood learned not to drink the water from the faucet. It was deadly. An accident had poisoned Flint's water, but nobody did anything to clean it. Nobody in the government seemed to care. Mari Copeny thought clean water was a basic human right, so she decided to do something about it.

In 2016, she wrote a letter to President Barack Obama to ask for help. Her mom told her that the president of the United States gets thousands of letters a day and Mari's wouldn't be read. But Mari was tired of being ignored.

And do you know what? President Obama replied! He came to see Mari and gave Flint the money needed to clean up its water supply.

MARI COPENY WAS EIGHT YEARS OLD AND SHE STOOD UP BY REFUSING TO BE IGNORED.

Each of these women changed the world for the better. But they weren't alone. There were many more who took a stand in their own lives in their own way, and there will be many more to come.

So now I've got a question for you.
When you look at your world,
what do you see?
What's the good?
What's the bad?
What do you love?
How would you help?
What's the change you wish could happen?

Whatever it is, it will start when you take a

STAND

Now, I'm not going to lie to you. It won't be easy.
Standing up means making yourself stand out from the crowd.
It means being different.
People might try to put you down.

But did Rosa Parks give up when she got arrested?
Did Ida B. Wells give up when an angry mob
burned her printing press to the ground?
When people screamed at Ruby Bridges, did she
turn around and go home?
No, they **STOOD UP!**

Remember this.
When you stand up for what you believe,
you don't stand alone.
You're standing on the shoulders of the
mighty ones who came before you.
So don't back down.
History has your back.

Now it's your turn. Don't be shy.

STAND UP!

For yourself.

STAND UP!

For others.

STAND UP!

For what you believe.

STAND UP!

To be counted.

STAND UP!

To be the change you want to see.
And if you do that, then believe me when I tell you this . . .

YOU WILL BE **MIGHTY**.

YOU'RE GOING TO CHANGE THE WORLD.

"WHEN IT COMES TO JUSTICE, THERE IS NO EASY WAY TO GET IT. YOU CAN'T SUGARCOAT IT. YOU HAVE TO TAKE A STAND AND SAY, 'THIS IS NOT RIGHT.'"
—CLAUDETTE COLVIN

Dear Reader,

I believe that Black girls are magic.

The very first book I read about a woman who looked like me was a biography of the great Rosa Parks. I loved that story so much that I asked my teacher for our fourth-grade class play to be about the Montgomery Bus Boycott. I got to play Rosa!

Growing up as a little Black girl in the South, I never thought I could fight racism, much less defeat it. But in that book and up on that stage, I learned that there were mighty, inspiring Black women who had confronted the beast head-on.

Rosa Parks taught me to shine.

I don't know that I ever would have become a storyteller without her. So here I am, sharing the stories of some of the many women and girls who have inspired me ever since I first learned about Rosa Parks's story over 30 years ago.